I0821313

Australia

Heather DiLorenzo Williams and Warren Rylands

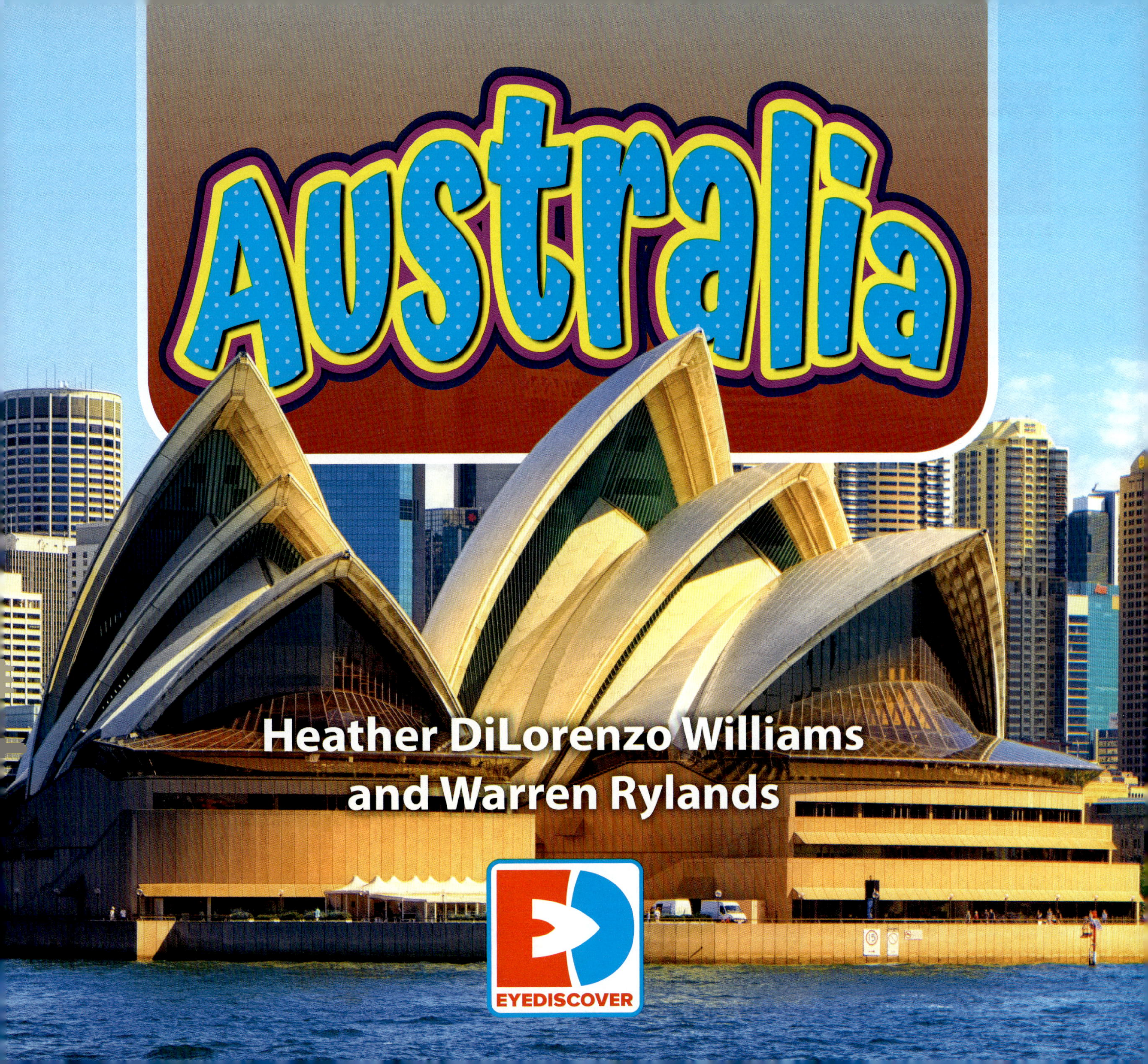

Go to www.eyediscover.com and enter this book's unique code.

BOOK CODE

AVZ95954

EYEDISCOVER brings you optic readalongs that support active learning.

Published by AV² by Weigl
350 5th Avenue, 59th Floor New York, NY 10118
Website: www.eyediscover.com

Library of Congress Control Number: 2018953514

ISBN 978-1-4896-8333-5 (hardcover)

Printed in the United States of America
in Brainerd, Minnesota
1 2 3 4 5 6 7 8 9 0 22 21 20 19 18

082018
120917

Project Coordinator: John Willis
Designer: Mandy Christiansen

Weigl acknowledges Alamy, Getty Images, and iStock as the primary image suppliers for this title.

EYEDISCOVER provides enriched content, optimized for tablet use, that supplements and complements this book. EYEDISCOVER books strive to create inspired learning and engage young minds in a total learning experience.

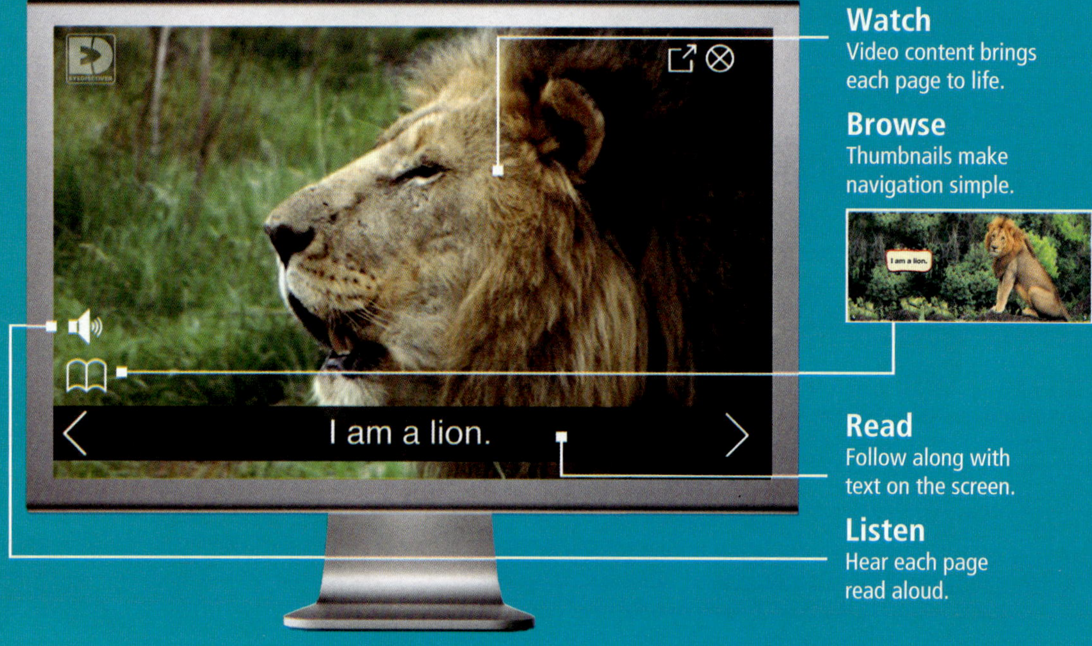

Your EYEDISCOVER Optic Readalongs come alive with...

Audio
Listen to the entire book read aloud.

Video
High resolution videos turn each spread into an optic readalong.

OPTIMIZED FOR

- ✓ TABLETS
- ✓ WHITEBOARDS
- ✓ COMPUTERS
- ✓ AND MUCH MORE!

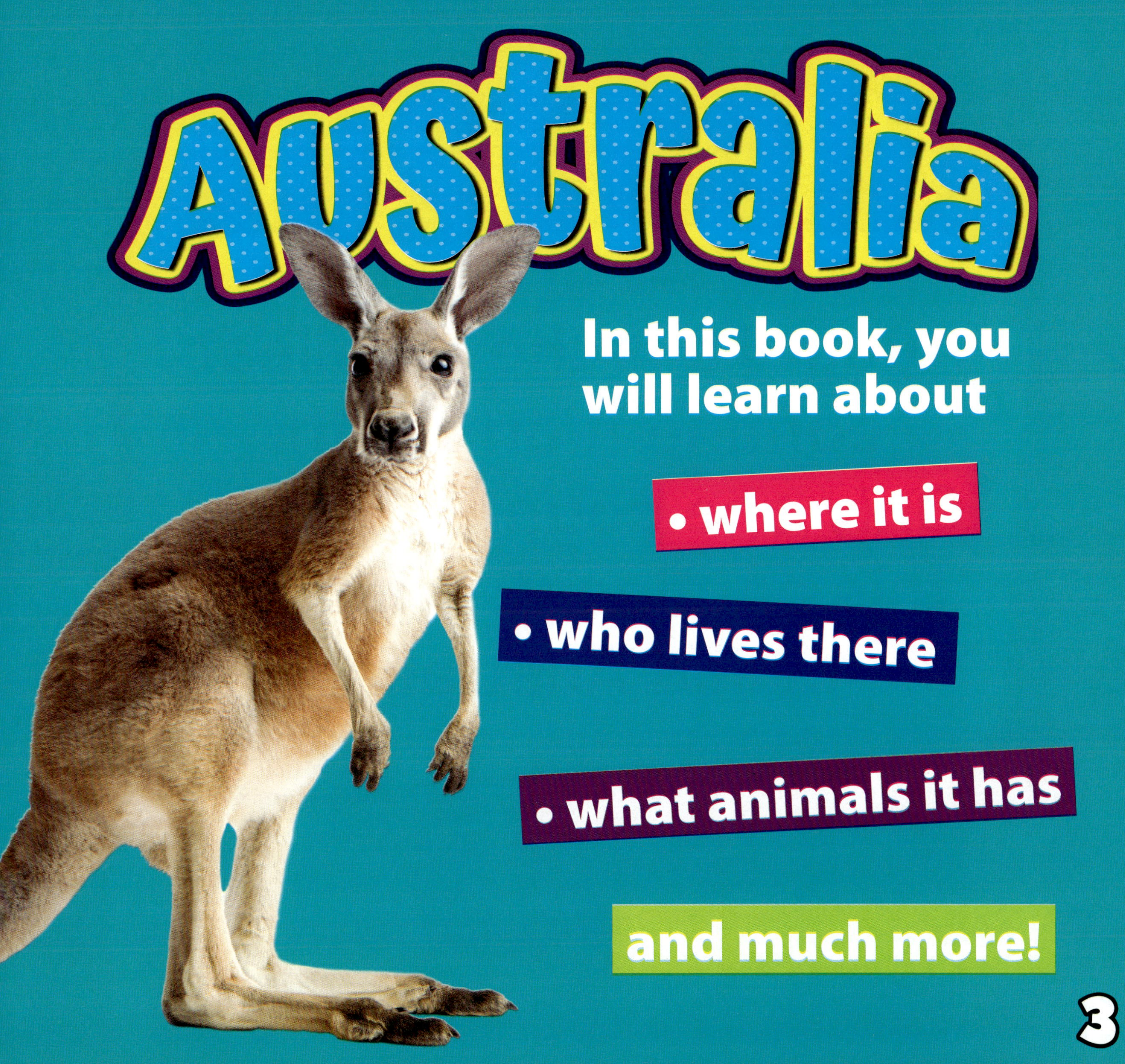

Australia

In this book, you will learn about

- where it is
- who lives there
- what animals it has

and much more!

Australia is the smallest continent on Earth. Only one country covers this continent. It is also called Australia.

Australia's native peoples have lived there for at least 50,000 years.

Today, more than 24 million people live in Australia.

The middle of Australia is a large desert. Most Australians live on the coast.

The city in Australia with the most people is Sydney. About 5.1 million people live there.

OPERA BAR

Australia has many unique animals. The kangaroo can jump up to 10 feet (3 meters) high.

More than 750 types of reptiles live in Australia. This is more than any other country.

Australia's Great Barrier Reef is the world's largest coral reef system. Dolphins, seahorses, and even crocodiles live there.

Australia is a beautiful continent, filled with interesting people and wildlife.

The **Great Barrier Reef** is so large it can be seen from space.

In **Australia**, about **85 percent** of people live within **30 miles** of the coast. (50 kilometers)

There are about **three times** more **sheep** than **people** in Australia.

Kangaroos can jump

25 feet

in a single leap.

(7.6 meters)

The **longest** straight road in the world is in Australia. It is

91.1 miles long.

(146.6 km)

21

of the **most venomous snakes** in the world are found in **Australia.**

KEY WORDS

Research has shown that as much as 65 percent of all written material published in English is made up of 300 words. These 300 words cannot be taught using pictures or learned by sounding them out. They must be recognized by sight. This book contains 41 common sight words to help young readers improve their reading fluency and comprehension. This book also teaches young readers several important content words, such as proper nouns. These words are paired with pictures to aid in learning and improve understanding.

Page	Sight Words First Appearance
4	also, country, Earth, is, it, on, one, only, the, this
7	at, for, have, there, years
8	in, live, more, people, than
11	a, large, most, of
12	about, city, with
15	animals, can, feet, has, high, many, to, up
16	any, other
19	and, even, great, world

Page	Content Words First Appearance
4	Australia, continent, country
5	native
11	desert, coast
12	city, Sydney
15	kangaroo
16	reptiles
19	coral, crocodiles, dolphins, Great Barrier Reef, seahorses
20	wildlife

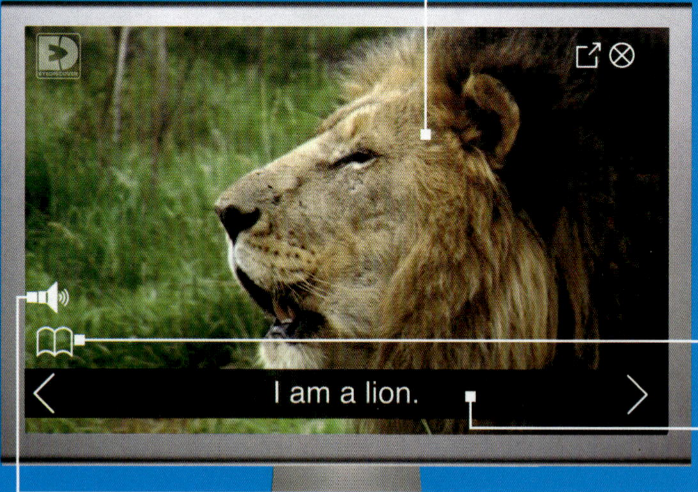

Watch
Video content brings each page to life.

Browse
Thumbnails make navigation simple.

Read
Follow along with text on the screen.

Listen
Hear each page read aloud.

Go to www.eyediscover.com and enter this book's unique code.

BOOK CODE

AVZ95954